Florida Manatee

Rod Theodorou

Heinemann Library
Chicago, Illinois

© 2001 Reed Educational & Professional Publishing
Published by Heinemann Library,
an imprint of Reed Educational & Professional Publishing,
Chicago, IL

Customer Service 888-454-2279

Visit our website at www.heinemannlibrary.com

Designed by Ron Kamen
Illustrations by Dewi Morris/Robert Sydenham
Originated by Ambassador Litho Ltd.
Printed in Hong Kong/China

05 04
10 9 8 7 6 5 4

Library of Congress Cataloging-in-Publication Data
Theodorou, Rod.
    Florida manatee / Rod Theodorou.
        p. cm. – (Animals in danger)
    Includes bibliographical references (p.).
    Summary: Describes the physical characteristics, behavior, and habitat of the Florida manatee and discusses some of the reasons it is in danger of extinction.
        ISBN 1-57572-265-8 (lib. bdg.)   ISBN 1-58810-331-5 (pbk. bdg.)
        1. Trichechus manatus—Juvenile literature. 2. Endangered species—Juvenile literature.
[1. Manatee. 2. Endangered species.] I. Title.

QL737.S63 T44 2000
599.55—dc21

                                                                        00-024323

Acknowledgments
The author and publishers are grateful to the following for permission to reproduce copyright material: BBC Natural History Unit, p. 20, BBC Natural History Unit/ Stephen David Miller, pp. 5, 19, BBC Natural History Unit/ Jeff Foott, pp.12, 16, 22, 23, 25, 26; FLPA/ Fritz Polking, p. 4, FLPA/ Jurgen & Christine Sohns, p. 11, FLPA/ David Hosking, p. 24; Mike Johnson, p. 4; NHPA/ Trevor McDonald, pp.17, 27; Oxford Scientific Films/ Nick Gordon, p. 7, Oxford Scientific Films/ Daniel J. Cox pp. 8, 14, Oxford Scientific Films/ David B Fleetham, p. 9; Still Pictures/ Michel Gunther, p. 4, Still Pictures/ Robert Henno, pp.6, 15, Still Pictures/ G. Veer p. 13, Still Pictures/ Fred Bavendam p. 21.

Cover photograph reproduced with permission of NHPA/ Henry Ausloos.

Special thanks to Henning Dräger for his comments in the preparation of this book.

Every effort has been made to contact copyright holders of any material reproduced in this book. Any omissions will be rectified in subsequent printings if notice is given to the publisher.

Some words are shown in bold, **like this.**You can find out what they mean by looking in the glossary.

Contents

Animals in Danger

blue whale

giant panda

mountain gorilla

All over the world, more than 10,000 animal
species are in danger. Some are in danger because
their homes are being destroyed. Many are in
danger because people hunt them.

4

This book is about Florida manatees and why they are **endangered**. Unless people learn to **protect** them, Florida manatees will become **extinct**. We will only be able to find out about them from books like this.

What IS a Manatee?

Manatees are large swimming **mammals**. There are four kinds of manatee. These kinds are the Amazonian, West African, Antillean, and Florida manatee.

Amazonian manatees like the one in this picture are the smallest. They grow as long as a soccer goal is tall. Other manatees are larger. Some grow to be as long as a minivan!

What Do Manatees Look Like?

Manatees are dark gray and wrinkly with very little hair. They have a narrow tail that they move up and down to swim.

Manatees have two small flippers on their upper body. They use these to help them eat and steer when they swim. They have nails like fingernails at the end of each flipper.

Where Do Manatees Live?

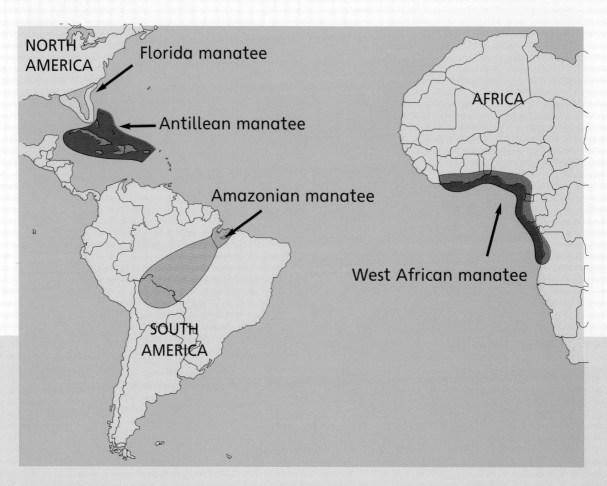

Manatees live in warm **tropical** waters. The Florida manatee lives mainly around the Florida **coast** of North America.

Manatees live in rivers, canals, oceans, and other places that are full of water plants. They can live in both freshwater rivers and saltwater oceans, as long as the water is warm.

What Do Manatees Eat?

Manatees are **herbivores**. They eat plants that grow underwater or near water. They use their front flippers and large lips to hold and eat the plants. They eat for six to eight hours each day.

Manatees eat turtle grass, **mangrove** leaves, and many other water plants. Sometimes the water the manatees are in is too salty. Then they have to find fresh water to drink.

Manatee Babies

Male and **female** manatees come together to **mate** in the spring. About 12 months later, the female gives birth to one baby, called a calf.

The calf stays close to its mother most of the time. It has to go to the **surface** to breathe. It makes sounds so that its mother always knows where it is.

Caring for the Calves

Calves drink their mothers' milk underwater. After a few weeks they begin to eat plants with the milk. They will keep drinking their mothers' milk until they are one year old.

Calves stay with their mothers for up to two years. They learn how to find food and warm places to rest or hide. Manatees can live from 60 to 70 years.

Unusual Manatee Facts

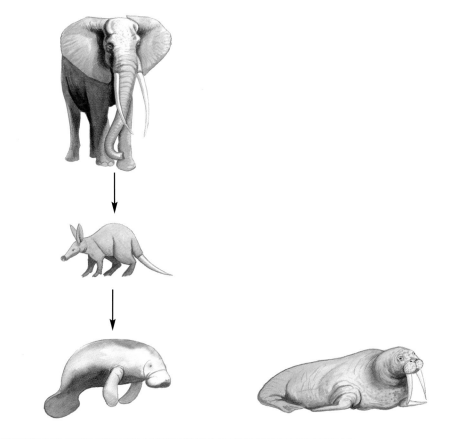

Scientists once thought that manatees were related to walruses. This is because they look a little like walruses. We now know that they are more closely related to elephants and **aardvarks!**

Manatees can hold their breath and stay underwater for 30 minutes. They usually only stay under for two or three minutes.

How Many Florida Manatees Are There?

It is very difficult to find out how many manatees are alive in the world today. We do know there are far fewer than there were 100 years ago.

Scientists think that there are only about 2,000 Florida manatees left. All types of manatees are **endangered** species.

Why Are Florida Manatees in Danger?

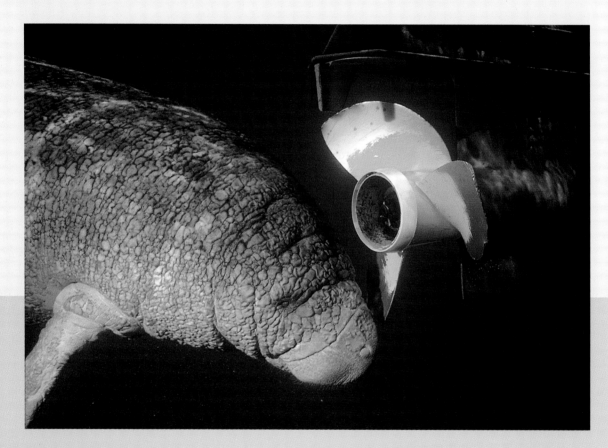

Florida manatees are very slow swimmers. They are hard to see in the water. Many are injured and killed by motorboats and ships every year.

Manatees sometimes swim into **lockgates** and get trapped and crushed. Some people hunt manatees for food or as a sport. Manatee hunting is against the **law** in most countries where manatees live.

Florida manatees need to live in warm water. A sudden, harsh winter can turn the water cold and kill many manatees.

There has been a lot of building in manatee **habitats**. The manatee is losing its food supply and its home.

How Is the Florida Manatee Being Helped?

Manatees are **protected** by **law**. In Florida there are laws so people can't drive motorboats too fast in manatee areas. **Conservation** groups raise money to buy land to use for manatee **reserves**.

Conservation groups also try to stop the building in manatee areas. Conservation workers check on the manatees regularly to make sure they are healthy.

Florida Manatee Fact File

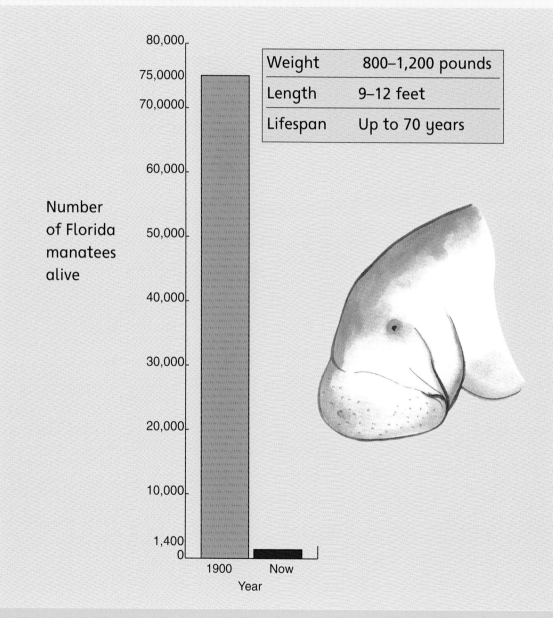

Weight	800–1,200 pounds
Length	9–12 feet
Lifespan	Up to 70 years

Number of Florida manatees alive

80,000
75,0000
70,0000
60,000
50,000
40,000
30,000
20,000
10,000
1,400
0

1900   Now

Year

World Danger Table

	Number that may have been alive 100 years ago	Number that may be alive today
Giant panda	65,000	650
Bengal tiger	100,000	4,500
Blue whale	335,000	4,000
Black rhino	1,000,000	2,000
Mountain gorilla	85,000	500

There are thousands of other animals in the world that are in danger of becoming **extinct**. This table shows some of these animals.

HOw Can You Help the Florida Manatee?

If you and your friends raise money for the Florida manatee you can send it to the these organizations. They take the money and use it to buy land, to pay conservation workers, and to buy tools to help save the Florida manatee.

Defenders of Wildlife
1101 Fourteenth Street, N.W. #1400
Washington, DC 20005

Save the Manatee Club
500 N. Maitland Ave.
Maitland, FL 32751

World Wildlife Fund
1250 Twenty-fourth Street
Washington, DC 2077-7180

More Books to Read

Barton, Miles. *Vanishing Species*. Danbury, Conn.: Franklin Watts, 1997.

Fichter, George S. *Endangered Animals*. New York: Golden Books Publishing Company, 1995.

National Wildlife Federation Staff. *Endangered Species: Wild and Rare*. Broomall, Penn.: Chelsea House Publishers, 1999. An older reader can help you with this book.

Glossary

aardvark	animal with a long snout, large ears, and a long tail
coast	where the land meets the ocean
conservation	looking after things, especially if they are in danger
endangered	group of animals that is dying out, so there are few left
extinct	group of animals that has completely died out and can never live again
female	girl or woman
habitat	home or place where something lives
law	rule or something you have to do
lockgate	gates in a river or canal that separate different levels of water
male	boy or man
mammal	warm-blooded animals, like humans, that feed their young on the mother's milk
mangrove	small tree that grows in water near warm beaches
mate	when a male animal and a female animal come together to make baby animals
protected	kept safe
reserve	park or large area with guards that look after the animals
species	group of living things that are very similar
surface	top of the water
tropical	place where the weather is hot and wet

Index